A Young Citizen's Guide To:

Parliament

Nathaniel Harris

W
HODDER
Wayland

A Young Citizen's Guide series

Parliament
Local Government
The Electoral System
Central Government
The Criminal Justice System
Voluntary Groups
The Media in Politics
The European Union

© Copyright 2001 Hodder Wayland

Published in Great Britain in 2001 by Hodder Wayland,
a division of Hodder Children's Books

Editor: Patience Coster
Series editor: Alex Woolf
Series design: Simon Borrough
Artwork: Stefan Chabluk
Picture research: Liz Gogerly/Glass Onion Pictures
Consultant: Dr Stephen Coleman

British Library Cataloguing in Publication Data
Harris, Nathaniel, 1937-
A young citizen's guide to Parliament
1. Great Britain. Parliament
I. Title
328.4'1

ISBN 0 7502 3774 0

Printed in Hong Kong by Wing King Tong Co. Ltd.

Hodder Children's Books,
a division of Hodder Headline
Limited, 338 Euston Road,
London NW1 3BH

Picture acknowledgements:
the publisher would like to thank
the following for permission to
reproduce their pictures: Camera
Press 17 (top); Camera Press/Jim
Cochrane 5; Camera
Press/Charles Green 14; Camera
Press/Stewart Mark/ROTA 8;
Camera Press/Don McPhee 17
(bottom); Mary Evans Picture
Library 9, 10-11 (centre); Eye
Ubiquitous/Howard Brundrett 29;
Format Photographers 23;
Photofusion/G Montgomery 24;
Popperfoto 12, 16;
Popperfoto/Duncan Willets 4;
Popperfoto/Reuters *contents
page*, 10-11 (bottom), 19, 25
(bottom), 26-7, 28; Press
Association/Topham 7, 18, 22, 25
(top); Topham Picturepoint 10-11
(top), 13, 15, 20, 21, 27.

Cover: Westminster Bridge, Big
Ben and the Houses of Parliament
(Images Colour Library); the
chamber of the House of
Commons (House of Commons
Library).

Contents

One of the great sights of London is a very large, long building that stands beside the River Thames, in an area called Westminster. The correct name of the building is the Palace of Westminster, but nowadays everybody calls it the Houses of Parliament. This is because two assemblies, the House of Commons and the House of Lords, hold their meetings in the palace. The members of the Commons are elected. But members of the Lords sit in their House because they hold titles (such as Earl or Baron) by inheritance or appointment. The House of Commons and the House of Lords meet separately, but together they make up Parliament.

A sovereign parliament

Parliament has played a central role in British history. It is the supreme law-making body, or legislature, in the United Kingdom – that is, Great Britain (England, Wales and Scotland) and Northern Ireland. When a proposed law, called a bill, has been discussed and agreed by the Commons and the Lords, it is sent to the Queen; once she has signed the document containing its details, it becomes a law, also known as a statute or Act of Parliament.

The Palace of Westminster in London. This is where the two Houses of Parliament, the Commons and the Lords, meet. Beside the Palace stands the famous clock, Big Ben.

Parliament can legislate – make laws – on any subject, without any restrictions, for the entire UK. And once a law has been passed, any earlier law or custom that conflicts with it is cancelled. This situation is described as the supremacy, or sovereignty, of Parliament. Of course, other bodies, such as town and county councils, make laws or regulations, but this is because Parliament gives them the authority to do so.

To become law, a bill must be passed by both the Commons and the Lords. Bills are passed, rejected or amended (altered) by voting; if a majority vote in favour (that is, if more members vote for than against), the bill has passed.

The Commons is much the more important of the two houses, and normally gets its way if there is a conflict with the Lords. The rest of this chapter is really concerned with the Commons, but the special character of the House of Lords will be described later on.

The principle of parliamentary sovereignty means neither more nor less than this... that Parliament has, under the English constitution, the right to make or unmake any law whatever; and further that no person or body is recognized by the law of England as having a right to override or set aside the legislation of Parliament.'
From A V Dicey, *The Law of the Constitution*, 1885.

Electing Members The UK is a democracy, so the men and women who sit in the House of Commons – Members of Parliament, or MPs – are chosen by the people. This is done by voting, which takes place at elections. The UK is divided into districts, or constituencies, and in each of them candidates present themselves, hoping to become MPs. All the adults living in the constituency can vote for the candidate they prefer. The candidate who wins the most votes becomes the MP and represents the people of the constituency.

Casting a vote. This man is placing his ballot paper, on which he has marked the candidate of his choice, in the ballot box.

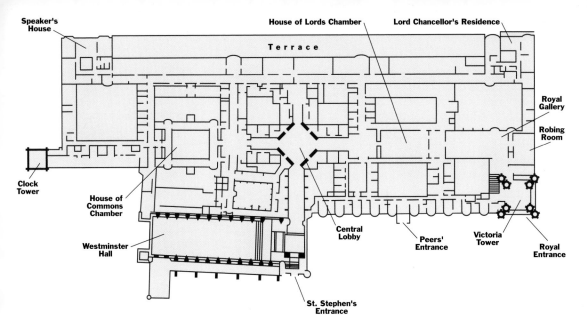

General elections, in which all the MPs in the House of Commons are elected, must be held at least once every five years. Most of the time people do not vote for an individual so much as for the political party he or she belongs to. Parties are organized groups that favour certain principles and policies; and, since people have conflicting ideas, there are many parties. Currently, the largest parties in Parliament are the Conservatives, Labour, and the Liberal Democrats. If the MPs belonging to one party outnumber the MPs of all the others, they can carry out the policies they want by passing or changing laws. Most people cast their votes in the hope of bringing this about.

Above: a floor plan of the Palace of Westminster.

Prime Minister Tony Blair and his wife Cherie (right). After the 1997 general election Blair became head of the government. The photo shows the Blairs outside 10 Downing Street, London, the official residence of British prime ministers.

Parliament and the government

Voting does more than decide which party will control Parliament and pass laws. The leader of the party with a majority in the House of Commons becomes the Prime Minister – that is, the head of the government, or executive. He or she will choose ministers to run the different government departments (Foreign Affairs, Trade and Industry, etc.); most of the ministers will be MPs in the Commons, and the rest will come from the Lords. So when people vote for Members of Parliament,

they are indirectly voting for their choice of a Prime Minister and government, as well as for the party they hope will win most seats in the Commons and pass the laws they want.

Government and Parliament are different things, but there are strong links between them. Governments develop and carry out policies and take all sorts of other decisions that rely on being able to pass new laws. So in the UK the government is normally chosen because it commands majority support in Parliament. If it loses majority support (for example, if some members of the ruling party break away from it), the Prime Minister and the entire government will probably have to resign. Sometimes a government has a tiny or unreliable majority, or no party in Parliament has a majority over all the others (this is called a 'hung' parliament). In these cases special arrangements have to be made, such as temporary alliances between parties, so that government can be carried on, at least until an election is held.

Government and Opposition

Parliament is not just about making laws. It is also a place where debates are held and the government's actions are examined and criticized. The supporters of different parties frequently clash, and the House of Commons is arranged as if to seat rival teams, with two sets of benches facing each other. Members of the government party sit on one side; members of the Opposition (the non-government parties) sit on the other. The largest non-government party in the House is known as Her Majesty's Opposition, and its chief receives a salary as Leader of the Opposition.

Front and backbenchers
In the House of Commons, the Prime Minister and the most important ministers (the Cabinet) sit on the front benches on the government side. The front benches opposite them are occupied by the Leader of the Opposition and other members of a team appointed by the Leader (the Shadow Cabinet). Commentators on politics often talk of 'frontbenchers', meaning members of the government or their Opposition 'shadows'. Even more common is the term 'backbencher'. This describes an MP who is not a member of the government or the holder of any 'shadow' post.

The State Opening of Parliament is a great ceremonial event that takes place every year, usually in November. The Queen is driven in her carriage from Buckingham Palace to the Houses of Parliament. She enters through the tall Victoria Tower and goes into the Robing Room, where she puts on the imperial state crown and a scarlet robe. Then she walks in procession down the royal gallery to take her place on a throne in the House of Lords. Once the Queen and peers (members of the Lords) are present, an officer of the Lords, Black Rod, summons the Commons, whose Members crowd into the back of the chamber. Then the Queen reads the Speech from the throne, the royal procession leaves the Lords, and Parliament gets down to business.

The State Opening of Parliament. Queen Elizabeth II is reading the Speech from the throne to the assembled peers and MPs. This is one of many ceremonies connected with parliamentary occasions.

Pageantry and custom

This ceremony is typical of British political life in mixing tradition with practical affairs. Its pageantry looks back to the past, for example in the way the Commons still stand humbly at the back, just as they did centuries ago, when they were far less important than the Lords. But the speech made by the Queen is not just for show. She is not expressing her own opinions but stating what the government intends to do during the year ahead. Holding a long debate about this programme is almost the first thing the Lords and Commons will do when the ceremonial is over.

The origins of Parliament

The history of Parliament really begins with the Great Council that became established in the eleventh century to advise the kings of England. Its members were barons (great nobles) and the most important churchmen. In the thirteenth century the king began to summon other representatives of the community to attend the Great Council. Each shire (county) sent two knights, and each borough (town) sent two burgesses (leading citizens), so that both town and country were represented. The expanded Great Council became known as Parliament (from the French word *parlement*, 'speaking'). And when the knights and burgesses began to meet separately from the barons and churchmen, two parliamentary assemblies were created – the House of Commons and the House of Lords.

The king in Parliament. King Edward I (1272-1307) sits enthroned, dominating the proceedings. For centuries the king was more important than Parliament, and within Parliament the Lords had far more influence than the Commons.

One of the main reasons why kings summoned parliaments was to raise taxes when they needed more money, for example to pay for a war. By the mid-fourteenth century it was accepted that new taxes could not be levied unless Parliament gave its consent first. This gave Members of Parliament the chance to state their grievances – the things they felt were wrong in the way the country was being run – and ask for them to be dealt with before they agreed to new taxes. When the king was short of money, Parliament's 'power of the purse' could be very persuasive.

Parliament did not become a real force until the sixteenth century. In the 1530s King Henry VIII worked with it to bring about sweeping religious changes that needed the co-operation of wealthy and influential people throughout the country – the people represented in Parliament. From Henry's time, new laws were generally made by Parliament and approved by the monarch, whose signature was (and still is) necessary before an Act of Parliament became legal.

Conflict with the Crown
At first, Parliament generally passed the laws that the king or queen wanted, but later it demanded a greater say in making state policies. By the seventeenth century there were many conflicts between Crown and Parliament over religion, the rights of Parliament and other matters. In 1642 King Charles entered the Commons and tried to arrest five MPs. He failed (they had been warned and had fled), but ever since then no monarch has entered the chamber and a curious ceremony is enacted at the State Opening of Parliament to emphasize the Commons' independence. When Black Rod approaches to summon the Commons, the door is slammed in his face; and when he has been allowed to summon them, the Members make a deliberate show of casually and slowly leaving the chamber.

The conflict between Crown and Parliament came to a head with a civil war, the execution of Charles in 1649, and the establishment of a short-lived republic. A second political crisis, the 'Glorious Revolution' of 1688, led to a more lasting settlement. The Crown remained powerful, but Parliament was recognized as an essential part of

Top: Oliver Cromwell dissolves Parliament by force in 1653. The seventeenth century was a period of civil war and bloodshed.

Below: William of Orange and his wife Mary were crowned as joint sovereigns in 1689. Parliament's importance was now fully accepted.

'Gunpowder, treason and plot'
Some parliamentary ceremonies commemorate dramatic events in history. Every year, before the State Opening of Parliament, a ritual takes place during which the vaults of the Palace of Westminster are searched. This is because, on the night of 4 November 1605, a similar search uncovered thirty-six barrels of gunpowder which Guy Fawkes and other plotters had hidden there in order to blow up the king and Parliament when they assembled the following day. The plotters were Catholics who hoped to overthrow the Protestant-dominated political system. Fawkes was arrested on the spot, tortured and executed, and his accomplices were killed or captured. In Britain, 5 November is celebrated with fireworks as 'Guy Fawkes' Night'.

the political system. It had to be summoned regularly, lasted for a set period, controlled taxation, passed laws, and was free to debate policy and check on the actions of ministers, who were still chosen by the Crown rather than by Parliament.

It gradually became accepted that laws passed by both Houses would automatically receive the royal assent (agreement). During the eighteenth century the link between Parliament and the government was also strengthened. It became clear that ministers could only govern effectively if they could rely on the support of a majority of members, especially in the House of Commons. So ministers now had to be acceptable to Parliament as well as the king or queen, and they increasingly sat in one of the two Houses. During the nineteenth century, as political parties became close-knit, monarchs had no choice but to ask the leader of the majority party in the Commons to become Prime Minister and form a government. In effect, the monarch gave up control of the government, which was chosen by the electors when they voted for MPs.

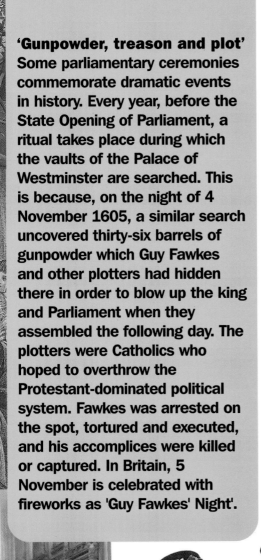

The Yeomen of the Guard search the vaults of Parliament each year. A ceremonial royal bodyguard, they still wear sixteenth-century uniform.

By the early nineteenth century parliamentary government had been established and England had become the United Kingdom. But Parliament itself was not a democratic institution. Most of the members of the House of Lords sat in it because they had inherited their titles from their fathers. The House of Commons was elected, but only a small minority of the population could vote. A long series of struggles gave more and more people this right, but it was only in 1928 that all adult men and women had the right to vote.

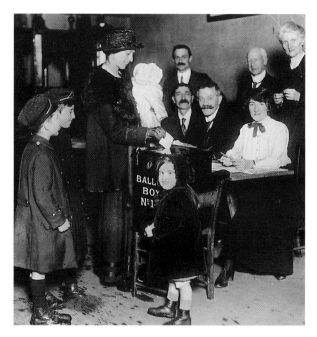

Meanwhile the second chamber, the House of Lords, kept the power to veto (block) most legislation passed by the Commons. Finally, after a great political crisis in 1911, the Lords' powers were reduced so that they could delay but not prevent the passing of a bill. Even so, there were, and still are, doubts about the part the Lords should play in a modern democratic system.

A historic moment. The year is 1918, and women over the age of 30 are allowed to vote in a general election for the first time. Everyone here is conscious of the occasion – and of the camera recording it.

'Parliament is not a *congress* of ambassadors from different and hostile interests... but Parliament is a *deliberative* assembly of *one* nation, with *one* interest, that of the whole; where, not local purposes, not local prejudices ought to guide, but the general good.... You choose a member indeed; but when you have chosen him, he is not member of Bristol, but he is a member of *parliament*.'
Edmund Burke was a great eighteenth-century parliamentarian and orator. This is part of his address to the electors of Bristol on 3 November 1774, and it describes MPs and Parliament as he believed they should be.

No Parliament can last for more than five years, except in an emergency such as a war. Some parliaments have had very much shorter lives, for example because the ruling party's majority was so small that the government could not get its work done. Whatever the reason, when the Prime Minister decides that it is time for an election, he or she will ask the monarch to dissolve Parliament; it ceases to exist and the government usually remains in office until the election result is known and a new Parliament meets.

Parliamentary routine

The parliamentary year is known as a session and begins with the State Opening in the autumn. There are recesses – periods when Parliament does not meet – which roughly correspond to the holiday times of schools and universities. The Leader of the House, a member of the ruling party, arranges the timetable of Commons business, which is published in a Daily Agenda.

Every assembly needs a chairman to control debates and give a ruling when disputes arise. The Speaker has this role in the Commons, while in the Lords the leader of the legal profession, the Lord Chancellor, presides. Both of these officers are accompanied by ceremonies that emphasize their historic roles; the Lord Chancellor, for example, sits on a seat known as the Woolsack, a reminder that wool was once the principal source of England's wealth. The Speaker is an MP (and therefore usually a member of a political party) but is expected to be impartial while in office.

Inside the House of Lords. The Palace of Westminster was rebuilt in the nineteenth century, with lavish decoration, in a style that was inspired by medieval cathedrals.

In the House of Commons, MPs do not address their remarks to the House, but to 'Mr Speaker' or 'Madam Speaker'. Fellow-MPs are referred to as 'my honourable friend' (if the MP belongs to the same party as the speaker) or in other cases as 'the honourable member'. A member of the Privy Council (a mainly ceremonial body of ministers, ex-ministers and other prominent political figures) is addressed as 'right honourable'.

Parliamentary procedures are so complicated that they are laid down in a special book that is over a thousand pages long. But essentially Parliament does three things. It makes laws; it debates important issues and government policies; and it looks carefully at the doings of government.

Legislation

Law-making (legislation) is a long-drawn-out process unless there are special reasons for haste. Almost all the bills put before Parliament are public bills, dealing with matters of national concern (private bills deal with specific local matters). There are two types of public bill. On ten Fridays in each session, backbenchers can put forward their own proposals. Known as private members' bills, these are seldom passed unless they are supported by the government, but they may publicize an important issue that has been officially ignored. Most public bills are put forward by the government itself as part of the programme outlined in the Queen's Speech (see page 8).

Even before drafting a bill, the government issues what are known as consultative documents, which invite comments and suggestions from MPs or people affected by proposed legislation. Then the bill has three 'readings', of which the second is the most important. That is when the Commons

Betty Boothroyd became the first woman Speaker of the House of Commons; she was elected by fellow MPs in 1992. She retired in 2000.

discusses the principle of the bill – that is, whether it is a good idea at all. If it is controversial, the Opposition is likely to attack it vigorously.

If the government wins the vote on the second reading, the committee stage begins. Committees play a vital part in the work of Parliament. A committee is a group of Members chosen to perform a task that would be unreasonable or too time-consuming for the entire Commons or Lords to take on. The balance of the parties in a committee is roughly in proportion to their strength in the full House. At the committee stage, the bill is gone over in detail by a standing committee (a committee set up specially for the purpose, which is dissolved when its job is done). The committee may report that amendments (changes) to the bill are necessary, for example to make some matters clearer. The committee's findings are debated in detail at the next, report stage, after which the bill has a third reading and then goes on to the Lords.

Members of Parliament file into the chamber of the House of Commons, ready to take part in a debate.

The diagram below shows different stages in the passage of a bill through Parliament.

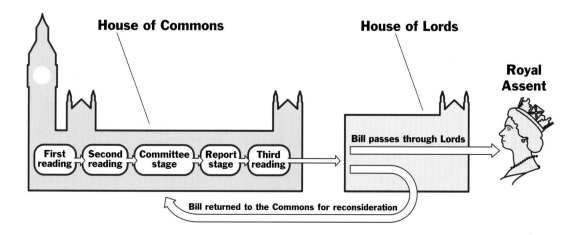

House of Commons

House of Lords

Royal Assent

First reading — Second reading — Committee stage — Report stage — Third reading

Bill passes through Lords

Bill returned to the Commons for reconsideration

Debate During debates, MPs put forward opinions and arguments either in favour of or against a bill or policy. Most of the time (but not always) the MPs put forward the views of the political party they belong to, but debating helps to make clear the strengths and weaknesses of each side's arguments, and to publicize both.

Debating is regarded as so important that it takes up about a third of the Commons' time. The first opportunity arises after the Queen's Speech, when five days are given over to debating the government's entire programme for the session. The government also arranges about fifteen debates on its policies, while non-government parties have twenty Opposition Days when they can choose the subject. These occasions tend to be dominated by the party leadership on each side, but backbenchers are given opportunities to launch debates at certain other times.

Persuasive speech-making, or oratory, is admired in the House of Commons. Here William Hague, the Conservative leader, makes a debating point.

Labour MP Peter Mandelson was twice forced to resign powerful ministerial posts because of alleged misjudgements.

Scrutiny

Parliament's other main job is to make sure that the government is not abusing its powers. This means scrutinizing (looking hard at) the actions of ministers and the departments they head, each staffed by thousands of civil servants.

One well-publicized way of doing this is by asking questions at set times when ministers are obliged to answer. Three times a week there is an hour-long Question Time in the morning, before any other business. Ministers' replies are worked out in advance by their civil servants, but follow-up questions may catch them out if MPs have identified weaknesses or wrongdoing in their departments. Further opportunities are offered, though only for half an hour, at Prime Minister's Questions every Wednesday afternoon, when the head of the government comes into the Commons to answer questions from MPs.

More regular and detailed scrutiny is carried out by select committees. Unlike the committees which consider bills (called standing committees), select committees sit for the entire life of a Parliament. They deal with a wide range of subjects, the most important being government finances and the activities of the main departments.

Non-questions

Prime Minister's Questions is one of the highlights of the parliamentary week. But Independent MP Martin Bell was disgusted by the way 'questions' from government backbenchers were often thinly disguised flattery. In his book *An Accidental MP*, he wrote that the event was: 'not so much a showpiece of democracy as a disgrace to it. Just when you thought it couldn't get worse, it did. Whenever I heard the phrase "May I congratulate my Right Honourable friend... " I would lower my head into my hands, dreading the sludge of sycophancy [grovelling flattery] to follow.'

Charles Kennedy, leader of the Liberal Democrats, the third largest party in Parliament.

How well does it work? The list of select committees includes a Committee on the Modernization of the House of Commons. The fact that it has been set up shows that MPs and the government recognize that the Commons may need to be reformed, or at least brought up to date.

However, there are varying opinions about what needs to be done. Some ceremonial aspects of Parliament are often criticized as wasting time or creating the wrong sort of atmosphere for a modern democracy. Recently, more attention has been paid to MPs' hours and conditions, especially since the election of many more women MPs in 1997. These have brought into question practices such as late-night sittings, which are hard to fit in with the needs of a family.

A more fundamental criticism is that Parliament, and especially the House of Commons, is under the thumb of the government of the day. The government draws up the timetable and has considerable control over the proceedings, if necessary using the 'guillotine', a rule that enables it to cut short a debate. It introduces most legislation and, through its majority in the Commons, normally gets its way. Even when some members of the majority party disagree with a government bill or policy, they are pressured to vote in favour of it or, at the very least, abstain (not vote).

Prime Minister Tony Blair with some of the large intake of newly elected Labour women MPs. The 120 women elected in 1997 represented a big step forward – but there were still almost five times as many men in the Commons.

Whips To enforce party discipline, both the government and the Opposition appoint reliable MPs as special officers, known as whips. Their job is to make sure that MPs of their party go to the House, especially when important issues arise, and that they vote as their leaders want them to. A 'three-line whip' means that the MP is definitely expected to attend, and a failure to vote will lead to a severe talking-to.

Of course the MP is free to disobey, but one who shows too much independence is not likely to be offered a government (or shadow government) post. This is a daunting prospect for young and ambitious MPs. Furthermore, a serious rebellion may lead to the withdrawal of the whip, which is like being suspended from membership of the party. And if the local party members in the MP's constituency disapprove of the rebellion, the MP may be deselected – not chosen to represent the party at the next election.

> **'Newspapers delight in perpetuating the fantasy that whips discipline members with smarting "raps across the knuckles". Occasionally it is true for MPs whose pride is enfeebled by ambition. For the wise and self-respecting, a haranguing whip is harangued back.'**
> Paul Flynn MP, *Commons Knowledge*, 1997

Despite the pressure that exists and influences many MPs, there are always members who are prepared to defy the whip when they feel strongly enough. In the past there have been issues that have split the ruling party, sometimes even causing it to lose power. As recently as the 1990s, the Conservative government led by John Major was certainly weakened by party conflicts over Britain's relations with the European Union (the association of European states to which Britain belongs).

Conservative 'Eurosceptic' MPs publicly opposed the policy of their leader, Prime Minister John Major, towards the European Union.

It has also been argued that government activity is so wide-ranging that Parliament cannot monitor it properly. At Question Time a relatively small number of answers are given by ministers in person. The rest are written, so that MPs have no chance to ask probing follow-up questions. Select committees have also been criticized as under-equipped for the job and possibly biased, because MPs of the ruling party form a majority on all of them. Still, the fact that ministers and civil servants often try to wriggle out of answering awkward questions suggests that the committees are not completely ineffective.

The House of Lords

The House of Lords has its own traditions and procedures. Some are very different from those of the Commons, but generally speaking the two Houses are similar, with government and Opposition benches, debates, votes and committees. The main business of the Lords is to examine bills sent to it by the Commons, approving them, suggesting revisions, or using its delaying power to make the Commons think again. However, some legislation actually begins in the Lords, saving the Commons' time. One special function of the Lords is to act as a court (the highest in the land), but cases are now heard only by the 'Law Lords', who are the heads of the legal profession.

Members of the Lords – peers – are not elected and never have been. Apart from Church of England leaders and certain law officers, until recent times peers were aristocrats who inherited their titles and their seats in the House of Lords. In 1911

James Callaghan, Prime Minister in 1976-9, was one of several Labour leaders who found that abolishing the Lords was not easy.

the Lords' ability to resist bills passed by the Commons was reduced to a two-year delaying power, which has since been further reduced to one year. (Public finance bills cannot be delayed at all.) But even after 1911 the composition of the Lords remained unchanged. Wealthy and aristocratic, it was overwhelmingly Conservative in outlook. Such a bias seemed wrong in a democratic society, but agreement on reform was hard to achieve. One change, made in 1958, was the creation of life peers, distinguished men and women who were given titles but did not pass them on to their heirs.

Then in 1998 the number of hereditary peers entitled to sit in the Lords was reduced from over 700 to 92. Further reforms were promised, but it was still not clear what they would be. Abolishing the Lords was not a popular option, but there were serious objections to every alternative. The model based on inheritance was plainly undemocratic. Yet if all the members of a reformed Lords were elected, it might become a rival to the Commons, creating serious conflicts. On the other hand the alternative, allowing the government to appoint the members, was not likely to create an independent-minded assembly. At the end of 2000 the fate of the Lords was still undecided.

Absent without leave
In May 2000, Baroness Jay, Leader of the House of Lords, wrote that 'very significant' recent changes 'may mean that the House becomes more effective as a genuine revising chamber' (preface to *The Guide to the House of Lords 2000*). But in December 2000 the *Observer* newspaper ran the headline 'Lords too ill, old or busy to vote... ever'. It reported that 'Nearly one hundred peers failed to appear for a single vote in the House of Lords last year.'

New Zealand's Parliament has only one chamber; its upper house was abolished in 1950.

During the Parliament that assembled in 1997, there were 659 MPs with seats in the House of Commons. Each represented a particular area or constituency, and together they represented the entire United Kingdom. After the Labour Party's overwhelming election victory there were 419 Labour MPs, 165 Conservatives, 46 Liberal Democrats, and 28 members of specifically Scottish, Welsh or Northern Irish parties. Voting for a political party has become such a habit that there are hardly ever any Independent (non-party) MPs. But in exceptional circumstances one Independent, Martin Bell, was elected in 1997.

What do they do?

As members of political parties, most MPs are committed to supporting or opposing policies affecting the entire nation. But they are also expected to look after the interests of their constituents. Part of an MP's time is spent in his or her constituency, holding 'surgeries' to listen to local people's problems and grievances. MPs also attend all sorts of local events, making speeches, opening new facilities, and generally making themselves agreeable. Both the electors and the local party organization have to be convinced that the MP is genuinely concerned about them – especially if, as is often the case, he or she does not live in the constituency and has no long-standing links with it.

At Westminster, too, MPs are expected to protect constituents' interests, for example by voicing opposition to any development that might lead to a loss of jobs in the constituency. MPs receive many letters from their constituents, and they often spend mornings dealing with correspondence in their offices near the Houses of Parliament.

Martin Bell, the first Independent MP in the Commons since 1950. He was elected on an anti-corruption platform.

Members of the government and leading Opposition figures spend much of their time devising policies and planning political strategy. Backbenchers may take part in the debates, vote and sit on the committees. If they are ambitious, they will try to be selected to put forward a private member's bill and will be active at Question Time.

Who are they?

The average age of MPs in 1997 was forty-five. Some of them had sat in the Commons for years, but most had had other jobs before being elected. Many Labour members had worked in teaching, local government and the social services. Business and the legal profession were strongly represented among the Conservatives. Some MPs continue to work in business, the law and journalism after their election, a situation sometimes criticized on the grounds that an MP's job ought to be full-time. The salary of £48,371 for a backbencher (more for ministers) was much more than most people earned, though arguably less than people in such responsible positions would receive in the business world.

'There were many of us in the lobbies aghast as we stood there and walked through. We had to do it three times last night, each vote taking 25 minutes. One MP calculated that he had spent 94 hours standing in the lobby during the last Parliament.'
Oona King MP, in *The Times*, 24 May 1997. New women Members have been especially critical of the Commons' traditional but time-consuming voting procedures, in which MPs 'divide' (literally) by marching into separate lobbies.

Less easy to defend was the fact that a large majority of MPs were white and male, although Britain is supposedly a sexually equal and multi-cultural society. At the beginning of the twenty-first century there were only nine black MPs and 120 women MPs.

Visiting a school. Most MPs take an active interest in their constituencies and try to raise locally important issues at Westminster.

During the 1990s there were signs that the British people were becoming disillusioned with the political system. Among the causes were political scandals and economic difficulties. But there was also a feeling that those who held power had too little contact with ordinary citizens and easily ignored their wishes. Many criticisms were directed at government and the civil service, but the popularity of Parliament suffered too.

A constitution needed? Parliament's

authority is unlimited, but we have seen that, for much of the time, governments control what happens in Parliament. So it can be argued that it is really governments that have unlimited authority. Some people believe this is dangerous, and that Britain should imitate countries like the USA, and adopt a constitution. This is a document that describes how the political system must operate. It limits what legislatures and governments can do, and guarantees citizens certain basic rights – for example, rights to freedom of speech, religious belief and assembly (holding meetings).

Agitating for a constitution. Members of the Charter 88 group gather to demonstrate in favour of their beliefs and recruit new members.

Because Britain has no constitution, Parliament can pass whatever laws it pleases. This has advantages, since constitutions can become out of date and stop useful things from being done. But laws passed by Parliament could also be oppressive, taking away citizens' liberties. When people begin to distrust politicians, limiting their power seems attractive, and since 1988 an organization called Charter 88 has campaigned for the UK to have a constitution. So far, however, neither of the two largest political parties has shown much interest in the idea.

The 'Cash for Questions' report, about MPs who had taken money from private firms for asking questions in Parliament.

Scandal and scrutiny

Probably the greatest blow to trust in Parliament was struck in the early 1990s, when it was revealed that some MPs had been accepting money from outside businesses and working in their interests in the Commons. After this scandal, the rules about how MPs should behave were tightened up and a Parliamentary Commissioner was appointed to investigate complaints about them. But final judgement on the Commissioner's reports was left to a select committee of MPs. Critics suggested that MPs might not be the best people to judge their fellow MPs.

While he was a minister, Jonathan Aitken had his hotel bills paid by wealthy Arabs. Exposed by the *Guardian* newspaper, in 1999 he was jailed for lying about it in court. At this time the media seemed better than Parliament in detecting wrongdoing by Members of Parliament.

Devolution While some people wish to limit the supremacy of Parliament, others fear that it is already being weakened in ways that harm the UK. In 1999 a new Scottish Parliament and a Welsh Assembly were set up. These formed part of a government policy of devolution (shifting some power away from central government). In theory, this did not affect Parliament's supremacy. Parliament passed the laws that set up the new assemblies and could, if necessary, pass laws that abolished them. This had in fact happened to an earlier, Northern Irish, Parliament, suspended in 1972 because of a crisis in the province and eventually replaced by a Northern Ireland Assembly in 1998. In practice, however, powers that are given cannot always be so easily reclaimed. People who opposed devolution felt that it would encourage independence movements in Scotland and Wales that might break up the UK.

European Union Britain's membership of the European Union (EU) has caused even more concern. The EU is an organization consisting of the UK and a number of other European states, which work together for economic and other benefits. It has developed institutions of its own, such as a European Parliament and a Court of Justice, and the UK, like other members, is bound to accept many of their decisions. For example, the UK Parliament had to pass a Human Rights Act (2000) which, by giving citizens the kind of guaranteed rights found in most written constitutions, is certain to have a strong impact on British life. As with devolution, Parliament retains its authority in theory, since it could always reject EU decisions or leave the organization. But in the real world that seems unlikely as the UK becomes increasingly locked into the EU. Fierce arguments continue as to how far this trend should be allowed to go.

A meeting of the Scottish Parliament, set up in 1999. The new assembly had limited powers but it soon showed that it would not always be willing to act as the UK government and Parliament wished.

Parliament and the citizen

Governments have their secrets, but the proceedings of Parliament are published in an official record called *Hansard*. Furthermore, viewers can watch the full proceedings on cable or satellite television, and extracts from some speeches and replies are broadcast on all news programmes. Commentaries on TV and in newspapers, though varied in quality, tell citizens a good deal about parliamentary affairs, and also about the views and activities of individual MPs.

However, once elected, governments and MPs are normally secure for the entire life of the Parliament (that is, until the next election). During that time, they may well come to think that what happens in Westminster – the centre of power – is all that really matters.

Prime Minister John Major (right) with Foreign Secretary Douglas Hurd at Maastricht, negotiating a European Union treaty.

Defeat: Conservative minister Michael Portillo loses his seat at the 1997 general election. He later re-entered Parliament.

Parliament and public opinion

So it will obviously be hard for an individual, or even a large group, to influence Parliament. Letters to MPs, complaining about government actions, are often simply passed on to the appropriate government department. But MPs (especially Opposition MPs) do sometimes take up cases of unfair treatment and try hard to see justice done. A tactic used by large groups is to organize a 'write to your MP' campaign, so that full mailbags stating the grievances of writers or farmers or pensioners will attract attention and make MPs realize that many votes may be lost if they fail to respond. Petitions, demonstrations, contacting the media and other forms of protest may also be effective, especially if there is wide public sympathy for the protesters' cause.

Public opinion certainly influences governments, and polls are now constantly conducted by newspapers and professional organizations to find out how people feel about different issues. Parliament, like the government it upholds, may take notice, or it may refuse to change unpopular policies if it believes them to be correct. If there are still several years to go before an election, government and Parliament may be inclined to stand firm, hoping to be proved right or to win people over. And in fact popular opinion can sometimes change very rapidly; in 2000, for example, strong public support for road hauliers' blockades, directed against high fuel costs, melted away in a matter of weeks.

A march by the Countryside Alliance, one of many groups that demonstrate when they feel their interests are being neglected by Parliament.

Though Parliament is not easy to influence, MPs prefer to be popular and are always aware that the voters can turn them out at election time. Scrutiny, criticism and publicity are the weapons Parliament uses to influence government; they are also the citizen's best means of keeping Parliament healthy and responsive to democratic pressure.

Activity

A good way of understanding how Parliament works is to set up a parliament of your own, preferably after visiting Westminster or watching proceedings on TV. Try organizing a debate: the subject need not be political but should be something you think is worth arguing about. Divide into parties and sit on separate sides of the room. Invite your local MP to come and act as the Speaker (it's worth a try), but if that isn't possible, elect one among yourselves. Find out and follow the rules and customs as closely as possible – even, or especially, small things such as not clapping speakers but making other noises of approval or disapproval. This will help to create an atmosphere very different from that of an ordinary debate or discussion, and possibly more fun. Good luck.

Glossary

Act a law passed by Parliament

adjournment debates half-hour Commons debates, held before adjourning (ending proceedings for the day), on a topic put forward by a backbencher

backbencher a Member of Parliament without an official government or Opposition post

bill a proposed law which has been put before Parliament

chamber a room; often used to describe the rooms where the Commons and Lords meet. The Lords is 'the second chamber'.

civil servants the permanent, paid officials who work for the government

constituency an area of the country whose votes elect an MP

constitution a set of fundamental laws or rules governing a country's political system

democracy a political system in which the rulers of a state are elected by the people they rule through a process of voting

deselection withdrawal of party support for the re-election of an MP

devolution transferring substantial powers from central government to local or regional authorities

draft the first version of a bill (or any other piece of writing), before it has been criticized and revised

European Union (EU) an association of European countries which includes the UK

executive the government, as opposed to Parliament (the legislature)

guillotine a procedure that fixes strict time limits to a Commons debate

Hansard an official record of what is said and done in Parliament

impartial not biased

legislature a law-making body. In Britain, Parliament is the legislature.

Lord Chancellor the head of the legal profession; also chairman, or Speaker, of the House of Lords

minister an important member of the government, in charge of an area of policy such as foreign affairs or trade and industry

multi-cultural consisting of many cultures. Describes a society in which there are many ways of life, religions etc., all equally respected.

Opposition in Parliament, Members belonging to parties that do not support the government

Opposition Days the twenty days when the Opposition chooses a topic to be debated

peer a member of the House of Lords

poll a count. It describes an election result, or an opinion poll.

private members' bills bills proposed by backbenchers

Privy Council mainly honorary body of leading government and ex-government figures

recesses 'holiday' periods when Parliament does not sit

republic a type of constitutional state in which there is no monarch; usually headed by an elected president

select committees committees of MPs. They mainly monitor government activities.

session the parliamentary year

Speaker an MP who controls the proceedings in the House of Commons

standing committee a committee of MPs that examines a bill after its second reading

statute an Act of Parliament

whips MPs who act as party officials, making sure members vote as and when required

Resources

Visits
Visits to the House of Commons can be arranged through your MP, who can be contacted at the House of Commons (Palace of Westminster, London, SW1A 0AA).

Information books
There are surprisingly few books about Parliament for young people. Moreover, modernizations and other changes since 1997 mean that older works may need updating. If this is kept in mind, the following are useful:

Stephen Coleman, *What Happens in Parliament*, Franklin Watts, 2000.

Nigel Smith, *The Houses of Parliament: their history and purpose*, Wayland, 1997. Describes the building itself, its ceremonial and the historical background.

Nathaniel Harris, *Crown and Parliament*, Wayland, 1996. Covers a crucial period (1500-1715) in the history of Parliament.

Nathaniel Harris, *Ideas of the Modern World: Democracy*, Hodder Wayland, 2001.

Stewart Ross, *The House of Commons*, Wayland, 1986.

Stewart Ross, *The House of Lords*, Wayland, 1986.

David Davis MP, *A Guide to Parliament*, Penguin, 1997. Probably the most accessible adult book on the subject.

Videos
Westminster Behind Closed Doors, Parliamentary Films, 1995.
Order, Order. Britain's Parliament at Work, House of Commons, 1995.

Fictional: *House of Cards* and *To Play the King* were very popular TV series, based on novels by Michael Dobbs. Melodramatic, but fun.

The internet
Quantities of information about both Houses are available on Parliament's web site, http://www.parliament.uk
Teachers and young people who need information or help can e-mail the Parliamentary Education Unit for information at: edunit@parliament.uk or write to the Unit at Norman Shaw Building (North), London, SW1A 2TT.
The Hansard Society, together with BBC Education, has produced a CD-ROM on Parliament and government.
Young people can find out about mock elections and other activities in the citizenship section of the Hansard Society web site, http://www.hansardsociety.org.uk

Index